Two women, Jill and Barb, sit at a table in a coffee shop.

> (Jill crying)

                              BARB
Jill….

> (Jill crying)

Honey ….

> (Still crying)

Jill …

> (Crying grows louder).

Jill …

> (Crying gets even louder, Barb hands her a tissue)

Jillian, honey.

> (Blows her nose loud.   Crying lessens)

Jill.

> (Crying lessens some more)

Talk to me.

                              JILL
He, he….
> (Blows nose again)
He's leaving me.   Charles is leaving me.

                              BARB
He's… oh … this is … I didn't know things were … I'm so sorry.

> (Jill still crying a little still)

What happened?

    (Jill crying a little less)

Did something happen to …

                JILL
He never really wanted me anyway.

                BARB
That's not – he wanted you – he –

                JILL
You remember the night he proposed.

                BARB
Sure I do. We were all out to dinner. You, me –

                JILL
David.

    (Enter David)

                DAVID
Hi.

                BARB
Sit down.

    (He sits, she stares)

                DAVID
What?

                BARB
Stop fidgeting.

                JILL
And Charles was there.

Goodbye Charles

A Play in One Act

By Gabriel Davis

gabriel@alumni.cmu.edu
gabrielbdavis.com

Cast
3 women, 2 men

Characters
Jill
Barb
Charles
David*
Andre*
Kennedy*
Violet**
Cynthia**

*David, Andre, Kennedy can be played by same actor.
**Violet, Cynthia can be played by same actress.

(Enter Charles)

My Charles.

CHARLES

Darling.

JILL

Who doesn't look at me like that anymore. Didn't even look at me that night that way.

BARB

Yes he did. I remember.

JILL

We wanted you to think he was … you were really at us a lot back then. Pressuring us to …

BARB

C'mon you two. It's been six years. You love her, she loves you. Isn't it time you two –

JILL

Yeah, when are you going to pop the question, darling?

BARB

Wait. Are my ears broken? You're backing me up?

DAVID

You aren't going to give her that speech about the superficiality of matrimony?

JILL

Maybe I'm tired of the refrain.

(She looks meaningfully at Charles. Everyone follows her, looks at him)

CHARLES

Maybe I am, too.

Holy shit.

DAVID

Stop the presses.

(Charles drops off the chair to one knee, ring box out)

CHARLES

Jillian, dear, will you marry me?

JILL

Yes, yes, yes!

(Ring comes out of box, onto finger, Jill looks at Barb)

It was a lie.   After, in the car …

(David exits.   Charles and Jill face front in chairs, apart from Barb now, Charles hands at   "wheel", they are laughing heartily together)

JILL

Did you see her face!

CHARLES

Classic!

JILL

Yeah, I don't think she thought we'd ever go through with it!

CHARLES

God after years of nagging us!
          (Car horn honks, Charles moves over a lane, laughing dissipates)
When are you going to tell her?

JILL

I'll call when we get home.

                    CHARLES
You think she suspected anything?

                    JILL
Why would she.

                    CHARLES
It is April 1st.

                    BARB
You never called me!

                    JILL
April 1st passed and then … it didn't feel like a joke anymore.

        (Charles pacing now)

                    CHARLES
You didn't call her?

                    JILL
What if … what if we went through with it?

                    CHARLES
It was supposed to be our joke.   That rock is glass.

                    JILL
I'm not worth making it a diamond?

                    CHARLES
Darling of course you are.

                    JILL
Then why not make it real?

        (Charles stops pacing, looks at Jill. Beat)

                    BARB
And so .. he did?

JILL

It was that or say goodbye.

BARB

So you –

JILL

So my friend Paul, the ordained minister, married us.

(Enter Paul, Jill and Charles stand side-by-side, facing Paul)

PAUL

(Pained expression)
I now pronounce you Man and Wife.

JILL

I thought it was the happiest day of my life. But it turns out Paul was right.

BARB

The minister.

JILL

Paul's been my friend since kindergarten. Back then he would follow me around the playground and fend off the other boys – so when I first told him I wanted to marry Charles and I wanted him to marry us… his reaction was –

PAUL

(Drops to his knees)
O Woe! Oh woeful, woeful day!

JILL

I figured it was that same impulse of his –

PAUL

Most lamentable day, most woeful day!

JILL

Just his knee jerk response.

PAUL

That ever, ever I did yet behold.

JILL

And I thought he was dead wrong.

PAUL

Oh day, oh day, oh day. Oh hateful day!

JILL

But in retrospect he had just the right words.

PAUL

Never was seen so black a day as this. Oh woeful day. Oh woeful day!

JILL

So will you marry us?

PAUL

Yes. I'll do it. But I can't stay and watch it. After I marry you I'm going to move somewhere far, far away.   Remote, where no one will ever find me. Pittsburgh.

BARB

Pittsburgh?

PAUL

I moved to Pittsburgh but left my heart in New York City.
        (Exits)

JILL

Almost as soon as Charles and I tied the knot, things started to unravel.
        (To Charles)
You haven't touched dinner, dear.

CHARLES

It needs ketchup.

JILL

You put ketchup on all my dinners.

                    CHARLES
I like ketchup.

                    JILL
Don't you like my cooking?

                    CHARLES
You never used to cook.

                    JILL
Are we supposed to order out our entire lives?

                    CHARLES
You never had a problem with it before.

                    JILL
Fine, I'll order something.

                    CHARLES
No, no.   That's ok, I – there isn't time.

                    JILL
Not the Cheese Club again.   It's Friday night.

                    CHARLES
Tonight is a grand tasting of cheeses from the Bosque region of Spain.

                    JILL
Can I come?

                    CHARLES
You wouldn't enjoy it.   I'll see you later tonight.

                    JILL
And that's how it went, him sulking around the house when he was there, and most of the time, out, gone, it seemed like his Cheese Club had an event nearly every night of the week and one night he came home very late, smelling of rose water perfume.

                                CHARLES
There are women at the cheese club, they wear perfume.

                                  JILL
And what? Rub it all over you?

                                CHARLES
I'm going out.

                                  JILL
At this hour?   Where? To her house?

                                  BARB
He's – he's having an affair?

                                  JILL
He didn't come back that night, or the next, or the next.   Then he sent
papers in the mail.

                                  BARB
Divorce papers.
        (Jill nods)
Have you signed?

                                  JILL
Not yet.

                                  BARB
Are you going to?

                                  JILL
I'm not sure.   I tried calling him. He won't pickup his cell.

                                  BARB
Maybe ... maybe you should.

                                  JILL
Maybe I should ... what? Sign them? Maybe I should sign them?

                              BARB

You're angry.

                              JILL

I'm surprised – seeing as it was you pushed me into this thing and now
you think I should just throw in the towel, say goodbye to years of --

                              BARB

I'm not saying, say goodbye. You've been together what – six years,
married what, a year?

                              JILL

Eighteen months.

                              BARB

Some guys freak out once things are official, you know.

                              JILL

So now, you – you who practically pushed us down the aisle – you're
advocating we what – end our marriage and start dating again?
        (Beat)
Help me understand this, Barb.

                              BARB

I – I –

                              JILL

What? Tell me.

                              BARB

Ok, um….um …

                              JILL

No, you know what – that's ok. I thought this might be a mistake and….
Thanks for all your advice.

                              BARB

Wait. Wait, Jill. I'm a hypocrite, ok. At the same time I was pushing you
and Charles to marry.   I was pushing David to do the same for us. After
all we'd been dating three years. So I started dropping not so subtle hints,

ordering wedding soup every time we went out, leaving bridal magazines in the bathroom, telling him I found him "engaging" over and over and finding other little ways every day to work the idea of settling down forever into conversation until he finally ... he finally ...

                              JILL
What?

                              BARB
He ran off and I didn't see him for months.

                              JILL
You said he was travelling for work. Some business in China ...

                              BARB
Cover story. He had some sort of breakdown, just up and left one night right in the middle of a dinner when he and I were out together. Bought a plane ticket to the other side of the world, I really didn't know where. His friends would only tell me, somewhere far. And he wrote me a note "I'll be back for you." What the fuck was that supposed to mean, right? Somewhere far. "I'll be back for you." He was gone so long....   I started dating again. And I'm out on this date... some guy I met online and ...
        (Enter Date, sits at table with Barb)
 ...and right in the middle, David, he barges in.

                              DAVID
        (David enters a restaurant. He is wearing climbing gear - looks like he came directly from a   mountain)
I'm sorry to interrupt your date, Barbara.
        (to Date)
Hi buddy, how's your date with my girlfriend going so far? Good?
        (In response to Barbara)

                              BARB
How did you –

                              DAVID
I asked Trish. She told me you were here.
        (to Date)
You don't mind if I sit down, do you? Thanks.

(to Barb)

Listen, honey...I can explain my absence for the last three months, really. I can. See. You're the most beautiful woman I have ever known. And that can be a little...scary. Look at this guy, he looks petrified. You know how three months ago, I kinda ran out on you at dinner? Of course you do. I wasn't being rude, I was being scared shitless. See, I wanted to, kinda tell you something extremely important. But I choked. Big time.

(beat)

I went home and, I cried, I wept uncontrollably, Barbara. Now that's not like me, I'm not a weeper. But there I am, reduced to whimpers, because I don't have the guts to tell you that I want you to ... so I turn on the TV, it happens there's this documentary about these guys who climbed mount Everest.

BARB'S DATE

Classic.

DAVID

(to Date)

Oh, you've seen it, buddy?

(Back to Barb)

So, I start thinking how brave these guys are, and why can't I be more like them.

(beat)

I mean those mountain men have stared death in the face, no way they would have been so anxious to ask if you ... See, then it occurred to me: I should climb Everest. If I climb Everest, little things like this, they'll be a cake walk. I know, I shoulda told you. But I just...went.

(beat)

The next thing I know, I'm trapped in a nylon tent at 25,000 ft. with a mountaineer named Gus. Winds over 100 mph are tossing grapefruit sized rocks and sheets of ice bigger than manhole covers though the air. All I can think about is you. I keep rehearsing this moment in my head, over and over...

(beat)

Every hour, Gus or I have to bundle up in our summit gear, crawl from the tent and shovel the snow into the screaming wind. If we don't, the snow will bury us, seal off the last bit of fresh air and slowly asphyxiate us. I keep thinking of this moment, with you. And in my head, this moment, it's not getting any easier. Somehow Gus and I manage to survive. Four days and the storm passes. We continue to the summit. The highest point on earth.

(beat)

At the top, it's breathtaking. You can see what seems endlessly in every direction, and there's this sense of being a God. I even made Gus call me Zeus. Then, staring out over my kingdom, I had this incredible, life altering revelation: There is nothing on earth more frightening, than a beautiful woman.

(beat)

I have looked death in the face Barb. Just like those guys in the documentary. And I have to say. Looking you in the face. Asking you what I'm about to... It's still harder. Barb, Barbara my dear, my love. (takes a breath in) Here we go.

(beat)

Will you marry me?

(beat, Barb doesn't say anything)

                                        JILL

What did you say?

                                        BARB

I was so scared, Jill. Here it was finally what I wanted, what I'd tortured this poor man for, and suddenly I wasn't so sure I wanted it.

                                        JILL

You love David.

                                        BARB

But what would it do to David? To David and I? He and I are so happy as we are, I thought. And I thought of you, of you and Charles resisting me all those years and how happy you two were until I ... because there were rumors –

                                        JILL

Rumors?

                                        BARB

You told, you told a lot of what you're telling me today – you told Trish then. The late nights, the weird behavior ...

                              JILL
I couldn't tell you – you who –

                              BARB
I know. But I heard anyway and I just didn't feel so sure anymore and I – I
said to him...
          (beat)
No.

                              DAVID
No?

                              BARB
I'm very glad you had this great epiphany, David, and now you think you
know what you want but ... but just because you climbed a mountain –
that doesn't make you ready for marriage.

                              DAVID
I am ready, Barb.

                              BARB
David, you ran off to Tibet without thinking.   I had to hear about it from
your friends, I had to read a stupid note "I'll be back for you."

                              DAVID
And I was.

                              BARB
Did you lose your job?   You can't just leave the real world for three
months, David.

                              DAVID
I can get my job back. I think ...

                              BARB
You're not ready, David.   This is not...this is not mature behavior. You're
not ready, you're not a man. I need a man for a husband, you
understand. Not...adventure boy.
          (beat. David exits)
So stupid. I tried to call him.   He won't answer my calls either.

                              JILL

You're not – you're not together.

                              BARB

It's been six months.

                              JILL

Why didn't you tell me?

                              BARB

Oh, c'mon Jill. You could hardly call what we've shared lately a friendship
– least not an intimate –

                              JILL

We have coffee.

                              BARB

Once every six weeks, it's easy to gloss over a lot of things ...

                              JILL

Ok, ok.

                              BARB

I'm not the one who dropped out of this thing, you know. I've been
calling and you've been screening.

                              JILL

It would have been really hard, Barb.

                              BARB

You blame me.

                              JILL

I'm sorry.

                              BARB

Oh, Jill, I'm sorry.

                              JILL

I know.

                    BARB
I want to get back to where we used to be – Coffee once a week, actually
sharing again -

                    JILL
Ok.

                    BARB
Ok.
        (Beat)
Are you going to sign them?

                    JILL
I don't know. I – we took longer than I thought. I have work.

                    BARB
See you next week?

                    JILL
A lot can happen in a week…

        (Women switch places)

                    BARB
So what happened?

                    JILL
That same day you and I met for coffee, two days after his divorce papers
had arrived, I come home from work. Charles was home when I arrived. I
hadn't seen him in nearly two weeks. He hadn't answered his cell in two
weeks…and there he was.

                    BARB
What did you say to him?

        (Charles is rummaging around things in the house)

                    JILL

What are you looking for?

CHARLES

You know what I'm looking for.

JILL

I want to know her name.

CHARLES

What name?

JILL

Her name. Why you're leaving me. Why you're looking for your get out of marriage free card.

CHARLES

Where did you put them?

JILL

I deserve to know who she is.

CHARLES

I just want to – to find the papers, ask you to end both of our misery here and sign, darling, and keep this as painless as it possibly can be. Please.

JILL

All I want to know is who she is. And I'll think about it.

CHARLES

Jill.

JILL

Just a name, Charles.

CHARLES

Cynthia.

JILL

Where did you meet?

                              CHARLES
Jill....

                                JILL
Where did you meet?

                              CHARLES
The cheese club.

                                JILL
Do you love her?

                              CHARLES
I care for her. Ok? Happy?

                                JILL
No.

                              CHARLES
Will you sign them?

                                BARB
Have you? Did you?

                                JILL
He was offering me more than half. Everything I came in with and more.

                                BARB
So you – you've signed –

                                JILL
No, no. No. I told him, I said – I ate them. That's right. I ate the divorce
papers, Charles. I ate them with ketchup. And they were good...goooood.
You probably want me to get serious about our divorce. The thing is you
always called our marriage a joke. So let's use logic here: If A we never
had a serious marriage then B we can't have a serious divorce. No. We
can't. The whole thing's a farce, Charles – a farce that tastes good with
ketchup.
            (beat)
I mean, wasn't it last week, your dad asked you the reason you walked

down that aisle with me, and you said "for the exercise." Ha, ha. That's funny. You're a funny guy, Charles. I'm laughing, not a crying. Ha, ha. I'm laughing because you're about to give up on a woman who is infinitely lovable.

(beat)

For instance: Paul. He has loved me since the eighth grade. Sure, he's a little creepy, but he reeeeally loves me. He's made one hundred twenty seven passes at me, proposed forty seven times, and sent me over two hundred original love sonnets. He sees something in me, Charles. And he writes it down, in metered verse!

(beat)

And that's not something you just find everyday. Someone who really loves everything about who you are as a person. Paul may be insane, but I value his feelings for me.

(beat)

I would never ask him to sign his name to a piece of paper promising to just turn off his feelings for me forever. But that's what you're asking me to do, for you. To sign away my right to...to that sweet voice Charles, those baby brown eyes, the way you hands feel through my hair before bed...

(beat)

Those aren't things I want to lose. In fact, I won't lose them. I won't lose you. I'll woo you. I've written you a sonnet. "Shall I compare thee to a summer's day. Thou art more lovely and more temperate, rough winds do shake the darling buds of may and..." I'm not crying. I'm laughing. It's all a big joke. It's very funny, Charles. I keep waiting for you to say "April Fools." Then I'll rush into your arms and... But you're not going to, are you? No. Of course not. It's not April.

(beat)

I, I didn't really write that sonnet, you know. Paul did. I think it's good.

(beat)

You see, the truth...the truth is, Charles, I ate the divorce papers, I ate them, because I can't stomach the thought of losing you.

(beat)

And then he just turned around

(Charles turns)

and left.

(Charles Exits)

BARB

Without the papers.

JILL

A day passed. I tried calling his cell. This time, no voicemail. It was disconnected. I got worried. I tried his sister's house, she hadn't heard from him. Another day passed. Neither had his parents. It had been three days by then. I was worried. Didn't know if I should file a missing persons or if he was safe somewhere, but just with, with –

BARB

This Cynthia.
        (Jill nods)

JILL

Unfortunately I didn't have a last name for her. So I did some research and found the name of the guy organizes the cheese club.
        (Enter Andre)
Andre Gerard. Owns a seedy little cheese shop in the east village.

BARB

Seedy?

JILL

When I stepped in, the place was kind of dark, dank and had this sort of, rotten smell … it was like the smell of …

BARB

Cheese?

ANDRE

Hello.

JILL

Are you – you're the owner? Andre?

ANDRE

Have we met?

JILL

I believe you know my husband, Charles and his…friend, Cynthia?

ANDRE

The name Cynthia sounds familiar.

JILL

They're both members of the cheese club you host here?
        (to Barb)
And that's when he told me.

ANDRE

I haven't hosted the cheese club for years.

JILL

I felt like I was going to fall over right there. Hadn't hosted the cheese club for years. Charles had been gone three sometimes four nights a week, gone, gone to a cheese club that wasn't.

ANDRE

Can I...can I interest you in any cheese?

JILL

No, that's ...

ANDRE

We have some very nice gruyeres. You can sample some if you like.

JILL

You said the name Cynthia sounded familiar?

ANDRE

Yes ... we had a Cynthia ... in the cheese club ... years ago.   Interesting woman, fiery spirit. Had a mean streak though ...

JILL

I knew I was grasping at straws, but I asked anyway – How did she ... smell?

ANDRE

Pardon?

JILL

Did she have a particular fragrance she wore?

ANDRE

Oh dear, that was so long ago.

JILL

I know it's a strange question. I'm – it's important.

ANDRE

I do recall a sort of floral scent ...

JILL

Rose water?

ANDRE

Yes, yes...yes, yes that's right!

JILL

Are you sure?

ANDRE

Oh yes, yes. I recall at the time my wife had become very fond of rose water candies and took to carrying a tin of them around in her purse everyone we went. When Cynthia would arrive to our cheese club gatherings, my wife, she would light up and greet Cynthia with this excited little shriek – "Oooh! There's my rose-water candy lady has arrived!!" And then she and that Cynthia would embrace. And they'd sort of rock back and forth together and my wife would repeat "My rose water candy lady, my rose water candy lady." Yes, in fact, I remember thinking how odd it was, this kind and soft side that this Cynthia showed with my wife, because with most of us she had a harsher way about her... Huh. Haven't thought of that one in years. Strange, the memory. Why do you ... ask?

JILL

My husband he's...he's gone missing. I believe Cynthia may be able to help me find him.

ANDRE

I see …

JILL

Do you by chance remember Cynthia's last name?

ANDRE

Oh…no. I'm afraid not. I'm sure my wife would remember it though.

JILL

Can you ask her?

ANDRE

No, she and I haven't spoken in years.

JILL

Oh.

ANDRE

Yes, she left me years ago. When she found out what I had done.
(Beat)
When business was good, at our height, this store was packed with the elite of New York City. Foodies from across the city gathered, wineries clamored to be included in our featured pairings, and members of our cheese club paid extraordinarily high monthly dues just for the honor of being part of our cheese-loving community. Unfortunately an investment banker by the name of Ponzl came into our mix and many of us invested large sums of money with him. It later came out he was running some sort of scheme, I can't remember the name of it now, but many of us, myself included, lost our life savings.
(Beat)
Shortly after the economy tanked. The cheese dried up … well except for the drier cheeses, they just sort of stayed the same. But the interest in cheese dried up. The wineries stopped calling. For a time, I had to close the doors of this cheese shop. We didn't know if we'd have a roof over our heads or a shop to call our own …
(Beat)
My wife took it hard … I could hardly bear to be there in that house with her anymore …
(Beat)
So I wandered the streets of Manhattan instead. A lost soul.

(Beat)
And sometimes, sometimes I'd walk into someone else's cheese shop ...
and this... this is how it would typically go ...
(To Barb)
Would you mind playing a cheesemonger?

BARB

Sorry me?

ANDRE

Yes, you. Would you mind?

BARB

What is a cheesemonger?

ANDRE

A purveyor of cheeses.
(No comprehension from Barb. Beat)
A cheese shopowner.

BARB

How does a cheesmonger act?

ANDRE

In this situation ... act terrified but also convey to the audience your deep
appreciation for cheese. Ready? I enter your shop.

BARB

Hello, sir! Ok if I have a British accent?

ANDRE

Sure, sure.
(Beat, Andre takes holds through the pocket of his blazer what
appears to be a gun)
Keep your hands above the counter where I can see them. No one is
going to die if you just keep calm and recommend superb cheeses.

BARB

Here you are sir, some cheese for you sir.

ANDRE

Oh thank you. I love Camembert!
        (Beat)
You know, I havent always been like this. Desperate. Knocking over
cheese shops to get a quick fix.
        (Beat)
I used to have a life. A wife. Like me shared my passion. Every morning
we would devour the triple brie on our nightstand, make love, and she
would sing this little song "aye, aye, aye, aye, I love new cheeses."
        (Beat)
And oh did we have new cheeses. Smokey vintage Goudas in amber tones
firm and flaky, silky drunken goat in striking violet tones decadent and
creamy, the most pungent of epoisses washed in apple brandy and aged
to nutty, meaty perfection.
        (Beat)
But then our fortunes took a turn for the worse. We couldn't afford
anything anymore. We hit rock bottom. One night, while eating a cracker
barrel cheddar, there was the sound of whimpering. We both looked up
in surprise. It was both of us, we had both begun to wimper without
realizing it. As time wore on the cracker barrel devolved into velveeta and
the whimpers into sobs. And I couldn't remember the last time I'd heard
her sing her little song....

BARB

Would you like more cheese?

ANDRE

Yes, all of the English Cheshire.
        (Beat)
I begged her to sing. She started "aye aye aye...". Her voice cracked. She
didn't have the heart to continue.
        (Beat)
I tried to cheer her up, but all I could offer was kraft singles.... She grew
listless, lying in bed all day staring at the ceiling.
        (Beat)
One day on my way to pick up food stamps I passed this wonderful cheese
shop. I stared through the glass my eyes bouncing like desperate pinballs
between a Roquefort, lindburger, and a taleggio...writer Clifton Fadiman's
words came to me "cheese is milk's leap toward immortality."
        (Beat)

As if in a dream, I walked quickly into the shop, my hand in my coat like this....back then I didn't actually have a subcompact Glock in my pocket, I assure you I do now...

(Beat)

I scared the heck out of the owner, and I came home with a board from heaven - Gorau Glas, Bitto, and Moose cheese. It was amazing, like Robert Deniro in awakenings, she came out of her stupor. She ate we smiled we laughed. I asked her to sing.

(Beat)

She started, aye..... Stopped too weak to go on.
The next day another cheese shop, another aye... Aye, aye...
Every day another shop another blissful board another aye until she was able to sing aye aye aye aye, I Lu...Lu....Lu....

(Beat)

We had hit a block at the word love. But I knew with enough high end cheese we could push through it... And I tell you sir, I feel that I am getting close - I am 27 cheese shops into this thing - and I am close to the mother-wedge that will set her free.

(Beat)

It will be sublime. Her voice strong and clear will ring out and I will rejoice as I hear her sing our song once more.

(Beat)

"Aye, aye, aye, aye, I love new cheeses."

(Beat)

Now put the rest of that Stinking Bishop in the bag and this will all be over.

JILL

You robbed cheese shops?

ANDRE

I did it for, for love. When she found out where all the cheese had been coming from, she couldn't accept what I had done. Couldn't accept me. The economy picked back up, business was never what it was but this little shop did survive. My marriage didn't. After she left, I never had the heart to start up the cheese club again....

(Beat)

I'm sorry I couldn't be of more help.

JILL

It's ok.   Do you know … where I can find her now … your x-wife?

                              ANDRE
I'm not sure, no.   I heard she remarried a couple years later. A man
named O'flannery.   Maybe you can find her – Violet O'Flannery.

                               JILL
Thank you.

                              ANDRE
I hope you find your husband dear.   Good luck.
          (He exits, enter Violet)

                               BARB
So then what?

                               JILL
So then I found Violet O'Flannery of course.
          (Enter violet, takes a seat).
But not where I expected her.

                               BARB
Where is she?

                               JILL
An insane asylum.

                              VIOLET
Hello.

                               JILL
Hello, Violet.

                              VIOLET
You're not the gentleman I was expecting.

                               JILL
Pardon?

                              VIOLET

It's a line ... from *Streetcar Named Desire*.   Blanche says it to the doctor before they haul her off to ... a place like this... I don't know you.

                              JILL

No.

                            VIOLET

They said my "cousin" Jill was here to visit... is that your name, Jill?

                              JILL

Yes. I'm sorry, yes, I'm Jill.

                            VIOLET

What are you, some second cousin twice removed?   Don't answer that.
         (Beat)
I know...just said that to get in, right?

                              JILL

Sorry.

                            VIOLET

Said that so you could come to gawk at the woman who thinks her x is a leprechaun, right?
         (Beat)
I've had reporters here who claimed to be relations to get in. I've had graduate students in here asking questions for their theses. And TV execs asking for rights to my story.   Oh yes, they come from far and wide to get a close look at me, at "her" - "The lady who found and lost her love at the end of a rainbow..."
         (Beat)
Why are you here?

                              JILL

I'm trying to find my husband.
         (Beat)
He's... he's gone missing and I believe you may know someone who can help me find him.   Her name is Cynthia.

                            VIOLET

Her last name?

                         JILL

She was part of a Cheese Tasting Club ....

                         VIOLET

My rose water candy lady!

                         JILL

Yes.

                         VIOLET

Oh yes, she was quite unique. A wit as sharp as cheddar, a beauty as
striking as green goat – the men in the club melted like fondue for her –
but her heart was as bitter as turned colby.
         (Beat)
You think she can help you find your husband?

                         JILL

Yes.

                         VIOLET

Why?

                         JILL

I think he is … I think they're involved.

                         VIOLET

If that's the case – and I do apologize if this feels a bit harsh – but after all
I am "crazy" – maybe he's better left unfound.

                         JILL

I need to find him.

                         VIOLET

If he's with another –

                         JILL

He loves me. He's just … confused.

                         VIOLET

You know my first husband really loved me but he was a lying cheese monger. One day he came clean with me about horrible, horrible crimes he'd committed and got away with to provide fine cheese for our family. When I found out that the road to put this cheese on my plate, though paved with good intentions, was tainted by the blood of innocents ... I ... I struggled with it, I did. I thought about – seriously considered staying committed to this man, who clearly loved me – but at the same time had also fundamentally betrayed everything our love stood for ... And I pictured our life together, our new life together in the shadow of what he'd done. And that thought filled me with misery and dread.

> (Beat)

A few years later I remarried Kennedy O'Flannery. I thought, here is a kind man, an honest man, a fact checker for the news. I thought with him, with this reliable, dependable man I will finally have someone I can count on. And you know what happened?

> (Beat)

This man, this fact checker, this man so grounded in reality ... a few short months after we married, he became convinced, absolutely convinced that he was a leprechaun.

> (Beat)

It felt like the floor had dropped from under me. It was happening again. Had another one lied to me? Had he just pretended to be sane for long enough to trick me into marriage? It was clear he still loved me.

> (Beat, enter Kennedy)

And he was working very hard to convince me his ... this psychotic break from reality was .... In fact not a break at all, but a real fact of our life, together.

KENNEDY

Why can't you accept I'm a leprechaun?

> (Beat)

It's like you're embarrassed. When we're out and I mention to people that I've recently transformed into a leprechaun, you always laugh lightly then veer the conversation to another topic. I don't want them to think I'm crazy either, but I can't lie about who I am.

> (Beat)

It is who I am.

> (Beat)

Look at the facts. There's a salary freeze but I got a raise.   The market took a beating, but my stocks are up.   Housing values are in the toilet, just not our house.
>   (Beat)
No people aren't lucky like that.
>   (Beat)
How do you explain that rainbow in our back yard? Rainbows do not linger for a week in low humidity.
>   (Beat)
I mean I get this isn't what you bargained for when you said "I do" But people change. Not usually into leprechauns but - and granted the priest said "do you take this man..." not "do you take this leprechaun..."
>   (Beat)
But this can't come as a total surprise. When you went on that special K diet and I went on that lucky charms diet...that should have tipped you off...
>   (Beat)
Or when I started to develop five o'clock shadows at 10 am. Honey this kind of aggressive beard growth is not natural...for humans. And I get you don't like it, how the stubble chaffes, and that's why I'm shaving every hour practically, for you.
>   (Beat)
But, cmon, you have to accept this.   We have to get it out in the open so we can work through it, together. This isn't easy for me either, I denied it at first too.
>   (Beat)
You know when I couldn't deny it anymore?
>   (Beat)
That day after my physical, when they found the sudden and medically puzzling height loss. I know the doctor explained it away as unusually drastic spinal compression, but I saw the look on your face, on his. And me, my stomach dropped out.
>   (Beat)
Remember how you comforted me. Said I didn't really seem much shorter. Still the same strapping man you married. But you towered over me as you said it.   I felt so scared. Remember I couldn't sleep...came to bed late...
>   (Beat)

But then, that night, when I came to bed, you were already out. I gave you a little peck and said goodnight - you said, and you had that tone, half asleep, you said- I love you, little fella.

(Beat)

Little fella. There it was the truth. It hurt. But less so because you were there. Snoring a little. Beside me. And you reached out and took my hand the way you always do. Because some things haven't changed.

(Beat)

I know it's scary.

(Beat)

But please, just accept it, even if it makes us a little weirder as a couple, please say it. Say - say honey I accept that you are a leprechaun. And then we can get on with the rest of our lives. What do say?

(Exit Kennedy)

VIOLET

I said, yes. I dove in and I accepted it – because, well because the facts really were irrefutable.

(Beat)

Kennedy was a leprechaun. And in that light, everything was ok. He wasn't insane. We both were sane, the world, everyone else – they were the crazy ones. And for a time, we were happy. Really happy together.

(Beat)

And then Kennedy started to deny our reality. He told me he was mistaken. He hadn't checked the facts properly. But he had! He had! I told him I knew he was right, he was a leprechaun, but he couldn't accept it anymore. He couldn't. And I – I just kept saying he was until – until he left me – but I kept saying it – he's leprechaun, my love is a leprechaun. It was around then ... that they put me in here.

(Beat)

I've been married twice, dear. All I found in that wonderful institution was deception and pain.

(Beat)

I'll tell you what, my current commitment – it's the only kind I'd endorse.

BARB

This is some pretty heavy anti-marriage propaganda. What did you do?

JILL

I just asked her again, if she knew where I could find Cynthia.

                            VIOLET
No, I haven't seen her in years.

                             JILL
Do you remember her last name?

                            VIOLET
Kennedy would.   She introduced me to him, actually.   He was an old
friend of hers.
         (Beat)
Be careful, dear.
         (Exit Violet, as she goes Kennedy re-enters, they watch each other
as their paths cross)

                             BARB
So you hunted down her x.

                             JILL
Hello, are you Kennedy O'Flannery?

                           KENNEDY
That's correct.

                             JILL
I'm hoping, you can help me.   I'm looking for someone, a woman named
Cynthia, whom I believe you know.
         (Beat)
I believe she introduced you to your, um, x-wife...?

                           KENNEDY
How do you know that?

                             JILL
You x-wife.

                           KENNEDY
You spoke with her?
         (Beat)
I wish you people would leave her alone.

                              JILL

You don't understand.

                            KENNEDY

Let me guess, you're writing a book or a paper or a tv movie and you want
my side —

                              JILL

No, no. I really just want –

                            KENNEDY

So that's how you're going to play it, huh?   You're going to pretend
you're not interested in my side of the story?
          (Beat)
Yes, it's true, ok? I was convinced for a time that I was a leprechaun. I'm
not proud of it. You know it cost me my career as a fact checker. My
insistence that I was a leprechaun. No one trusted me to check the
validity of stories after they found out my belief about myself.   And I did
not come to that conclusion lightly, but every fact I analyzed seemed to
point irrefutably to that certain reality.
          (Beat)
I became convinced, Violet became convinced. We lost everyone in our
life.
          (Beat)
My investment banker quite on me – too embarrassing for his firm, he
said. My stocks took a beating. The neighbors sold their houses in a
down economy and our housing value plummeted.
          (Beat)
I started to realize – all this bad luck that was befalling us. If I was really a
leprechaun would that be happening.
          (Beat)
I found out there was a mix-up and the pharmacy had been giving me
testosterone instead of insulin for my diabetes ... and anyway, who ever
heard of a diabetic leprechaun.   Not sure how that one had got past me.
          (Beat)
But the kicker was when our neighbor moved, and his sprinkler system
stopped for a few days ... the rainbows stopped.
          (Beat)
But she wouldn't believe me. She insisted.   She kept saying it.

                              JILL

So you had her committed?

                              KENNEDY

No, she actually committed herself, after she divorced me. I begged her
not to go in, but she told me – said she would only come out when I
admitted the truth. She lets journalists and tv execs and complete
strangers come visit her. But not me. No, I'm locked out.

                              JILL

I'm sorry.

                              BARB

Awkward.

                              JILL

So um …. this Cynthia woman ….

                              KENNEDY

Why are you looking for her?

                              JILL

I think my husband is involved with her.

                              KENNEDY

Oh.

                              JILL

Do you know where I can find her?

                              KENNEDY

You won't find her.

                              JILL

What do you mean?

                              KENNEDY

She's dead.
          (Beat)

It … it just happened a few days ago.   It was so sudden, unexpected. The police suspect foul play. They questioned the man who she was involved with.

                              JILL

They questioned him?

                              KENNEDY

He was the last one to see her alive.

                              BARB

Charles? Charles is under investigation?

                              JILL

This man – his name was Charles?

                              KENNEDY

She didn't tell me his name. Just that she was spending a lot of time with a married man. She was engaged to be married herself. But she said, she told me this other man she was spending all this time with, obviously behind her fiancé's back, she was doing it because he was "like her" …

                              JILL

What did she mean "like her"?

                              KENNEDY

I don't know I …   Look, Cynthia, she - she liked playing with fire.
        (Beat)
When I first met her – I was very young, fresh out of college, visiting New York for the first time, interviewing for jobs. And she was my best friend's girlfriend.
        (Beat)
He was bartending nights, so asked her show me around the city and I – we had this incredible time together.   I was smitten – one night I was … I got scared. So I flew back home but I couldn't get her out of my mind and then… then I did something crazy …
        (Enter Cynthia)
God, my heart is beating fast now, thinking of that moment.   How beautiful she looked standing in that doorway.

CYNTHIA

Kennedy?   What are you doing here?

KENNEDY

I'm ... I'm ...

CYNTHIA

You're what?

KENNEDY

I'm not the kind of guy who spends hundreds on a last minute flight back to New York, tears across town, then runs up six flights of stairs and knocks on my best friend's girlfriend's door in order to run off and elope with her based on one crazy, thoughtless, inexplicably romantic night.
      (Beat)
So what am I doing here, Cynthia? I'm not passionate. I'm a fact checker for Christ's sake. And the fact of me – being here – doesn't check out. It's nuts! Soul-mates? I don't believe in them. Never have. So how can I be yours? The fact is, you hardly know me! And I hardly know you!
      (Beat)
Now, your boyfriend, I've known since kindergarten. Am I really willing to throw all those years of friendship away based on...what? Some feeling? Some intense, aching, gnawing, burning, torturing feeling that's telling me I must be with you or I'll die a slow and horrible death as my heart slowly breaks into a thousand pieces? No!
      (Beat)
I mean, this is the kind of thing that only happens in the movies – and we're not in the movies. We're on McDougal Street, two blocks south of Bleecker – that's where we are. That is an indisputable geographical fact. A solid, rational, clear, black and white fact. And all the facts are pointing to one thing: we can't do this. All the facts say I shouldn't be here.
      (Beat)
Because the fact is you are in a relationship. Because the fact is we just met yesterday. Because the fact is I'm not the kind of guy who falls in love. That's a fact. A cold hard fact. And facts are supposed to be true.
      (Beat)
But the problem is....see...the problem is...despite every fact I can muster, there's something that still doesn't check out. Because the truth is despite all facts to the contrary...I still love you madly. And it just defies all reason.

All morality. All sense. But I do. I love you madly. And it's not like me. And I don't want to. But I can't help it.
> (Beat)

I'm yours, Cynthia. Completely, totally, hopelessly, and utterly...yours..
> (Exit Cynthia)

JILL

You two eloped?

KENNEDY

She wouldn't. But I got a job checking facts for the times and we saw each other in secret for some months. When the truth finally came out, I lost my best friend. We stayed together for a time, but I wanted more – I wanted her to be my wife.   She said she couldn't. So we broke up, but remained friends...

JILL

How did she die?

KENNEDY

Sudden massive coronary the day after her wedding. After she had a secret lunch...I guess with your husband.   There are some poisons that could cause it and ...

JILL

I can't believe my husband would have done anything to her. He's a lot of things but not... not ...

KENNEDY

If he cared for her. I'm sure he'll be at her funeral. It's tomorrow.
> (Exit Kennedy)

BARB

That's today.

JILL

Later this morning.   I'm going there after this.
> (Beat)

Can you come with me?

                              BARB

If you need me I'll ... I was supposed to see David today, after this.

                              JILL

He answered your calls?

                              BARB

He stopped by my house yesterday.
        (Enter David)
I get this knock on my door. I open it and there's...David.

                              DAVID

Hi Barb, it's been awhile.

                              BARB

Six weeks.

                              DAVID

I know.
        (Beat)
I've – I've been thinking a lot about what you said that night. That I'm not
ready, that I need to grow up, that I'm not a man, and you want a man.
I've been thinking about it and I wanted you to know, I think I figured out
how to fix that, uh, issue.
        (Beat)
My bar-mitzvah - my transformation from boy to man at the age of 13. I
don't think I got it right. I remember stuttering when I read the Shama.
And my chanting, especially during the Haftorah, as I recall my bubbie
telling me, it was a little off-key. So I'm thinking, maybe, due to that, I
didn't enter manhood properly. Or perhaps I missed the entrance
altogether. Or perhaps God locked the entrance, because he couldn't
understand the torah portion through my heavy lisp.
        (Beat)
Anyway, since then I've really grown up a lot. I mean, according to you,
not into a real man, but... I mean, I don't stutter, I don't lisp, granted I still
sing off-key, but...and then it hit me. This is genius. Brace yourself.
Seriously, hold onto the door frame or something: What if I got bar
mitzvahed again? What if I got re-bar mitzvahed? I could nail it this time.
Just knock that bar-mitzvah out of the synagogue.
        (Beat)

So I've been studying Hebrew. Went to a Rabbi these last six weeks. Been training intensely. I mean, Karate Kid training. Not just reading the Torah, but wax-on wax-off stuff like going to Saturday services, making Gefilte fish from scratch, learning to drive a hard bargain at the grocery. I even went back to Hebrew school and stood up to the current bully there. Granted the kid was like 4'11", but my heart was still pounding like crazy.
> (Beat)

And after all that, I can feel it, I'm ready. Ready for man-land. Ready to pay a mortgage and take out a 401k and sell insurance or cars or be a banker or something. And like, father some kids. I am charged. I am pumped. And tomorrow is my big day. Tomorrow, thirteen years after my first bar-mitzvah I am going to do it again – and it is going to rock!
> (Beat)

Tomorrow before your eyes and my families' - may Bubbie rest in piece - I will become a man. I will step up on that bema and you will WITNESS my TRANSFORMATION!
> (Beat)

So, uh, anyhoo...that's why I'm here. Just wanted to, uh, hand deliver this invitation to my bar-mitzvah. We're going to do a nice little reception after, we'll have a DJ, should be dancing part, maybe they'll play our song, or not, and uh no need to bring a gift, I know its on short notice.
> (Beat)

But, um...if you could just fill out this little card – chicken or fish.   Or not. Um...
> (Beat)

Look, you really don't have to say anything now.   I just … hope to see you tomorrow, ok?
> (Exit David)

JILL

You're not coming to a funeral with me. You are going to his Bar Mitzvah.

BARB

Are you sure?

JILL

Let's promise to meet tomorrow – catch each other up.

BARB

Deal.

(Women circle to opposite seats at the table, sit).

                          BARB
So ... the funeral .... what happened?

                          JILL
You first.

                          BARB
Well, the Bar Mitvah was at the New Shul. Yeah, he did a pretty good job.
Chanted on-key. Had the reception at The Alger House on Downing.
There was some dancing and we took more than a couple turns around
the dance floor together...

                          JILL
That's good.

                          BARB
He ... he didn't propose again. But he let me know – and I believe him –
he's ready.

                          JILL
Well then things ended ... happily ever after for you.

                          BARB
What happened at the funeral?

                          JILL
Charles was there.
        (Enter Charles)
Giving ... the eulogy.

                          CHARLES
I know many of you don't know me. Many you are wondering why her
father or mother or husband are not up here speaking. And also
wondering who I am.
        (Beat)
Unfortunately, Cynthia lied to most of you. Pretended to have a family
because the truth was too horrible.
        (Beat)

Cynthia's parents died in a tragic accident when she was only a child. And by tragic accident I mean her father accidentally killed her mother with a spatula while arguing over the correct way to cook pancakes. Distraught, he then intentionally took his own life with an immersion blender, however it can still be considered part of the original pancake accident. Anyway, it's not worth nitpicking the terminology – they're both unable to be here.
>   (Beat)
Her husband, well, he was planning to be here today, he was. However the police took him into custody this morning so ...
>   (Beat)
Guess I'm left.
>   (Beat)
Haha, haha. Um ...
>   (Beat)
I've actually only known Cynthia a little over a year ... But in that time, Cynthia, she and I had become ... very close.
>   (Beat)
I met her when I was ... actually the night before I was to be married ... my best mates and I were smoking cigars and sipping martinis. Cynthia was there ...
>   (Enter Cynthia)
She was ... waiting on our table. Whilst drinking my first martini an olive caught in my throat and
>   (Enter Cynthia)
-she hit my back and it popped right out. Why thank you.

CYNTHIA

No problem.

CHARLES

The second martini I had, another olive caught in my throat. She was there and smacked my back, but nothing happened. So she did the Heimlich. Out it came. Oh boy. Thank you.

CYNTHIA

Watch yourself, guy.

CHARLES

Sure thing! On my third drink I somehow managed to choke on all three olives and the little onion all at once. She tried all the tactics she could think of.

CYNTHIA
Nothing is working! Oh God – this man is going to die!!

CHARLES
The oxygen stopped flowing to my brain and … I felt it was the end and … I was not scared … I felt strangely … relieved.
(Beat)
Apparently, however, that same waitress, Cynthia went running through the restaurant –

CYNTHIA
Is there a doctor in the house!? Is there a doctor in the house!?

CHARLES
They managed to find a woman finishing her residency who with just a pocket knife and a straw managed to create a makeshift stent and keep air flowing to my brain until the paramedics arrived.
(Beat)
During the wait, I came to enough to realize what was going on. Since I couldn't speak I scrawled onto a napkin and handed it to the waitress …

CYNTHIA
(Reading)
"Tell them not to bother my fiancé over this."

JILL
Remember that huge bandage on his neck at the wedding?

BARB
Yeah, "cut shaving" never seemed credible.

CHARLES
She convinced my mates not to say anything – then told the paramedics she was my sister so she could ride along with me to the hospital. They sedated me and I fell asleep with this stranger holding my hand…when I awoke.

CYNTHIA

Do you have a death wish, guy?

CHARLES

It's Charles.

CYNTHIA

Yes, I know – it was your big night. Remember?

CHARLES

Does my fiancé know?
        (She shakes her head)
Good.

CYNTHIA

You're scared aren't you? That's why you tried to off-yourself with olives?

CHARLES

It was just an accident.
        (Beat)
But she was right. I'd never choked on a martini in my life – not until that night.

CYNTHIA

I understand, you know? I'm like you. I'd be terrified, too.

CHARLES

She scrawled an address onto a piece of paper and handed it to me.

CYNTHIA

That's the location of a CPA chapter. I think you might find it ... helpful.

CHARLES

You think a group of Certified Public Accountants can help me?

CYNTHIA

It stands for Commitment Phobes Anonymous. We meet Monday, Wednesday and Friday nights.
        (Beat)

You'd be embarrassed to attend?
>   (He nods.   Beat)
Tell people you're going to ….
>   (Beat)
… a Cheese Tasting Club.

CHARLES

The next morning I was … married.   From the moment I said "I do" I was terrified twenty-four seven.
>   (Beat)
My fear manifest itself as chronic irritability, which seemed to intensify with each new day of marriage.
>   (Beat)
So I joined the "Cheese Tasting Club."   It's there I got to know Cynthia.

CYNTHIA

Just a few weeks ago, my boyfriend, this lovely man I am seeing – he dropped to one knee.
>   (Beat)
You know what I said to him?
>   (Beat)
Don't do it! Don't open that little box one more crack! Don't ask me to marry you. Shh, shh, shh. Don't say another word. Just listen.
>   (Beat)
I can't let you do this to me. I mean, before I met you I used be such a bitch. I mean, seriously, everyone at work thought I was a huge bitch. No one actually liked me. Those people I introduced to you as my friends. They're not my friends. They're scared of me. Or they were...before I met you.
>   (Beat)
Before you, I never said please or thank you at restaurants. I never smiled or laughed at anyone's jokes but mine. I never used to tip more than 10%. I was quick with insults. I always had a cruel word. I was cold, cross, crass, falsely compassionate.
>   (Beat)
But since being with you, I've begun to feel all...warm inside. Fuzzy. I find myself wanting to stroll in the park and whistle!
>   (Beat)
I have these thoughts, these urges to donate to charities and help out in soup kitchens, and hug people. Since being with you, I've given nearly ten

dollars to homeless men, helped three old ladies cross the street, and I bought one of my so called "friends" a present at full price. And it was something I knew she'd like.

(Beat)

Don't you see? Don't you see you've made me NICE!? And what really scares me is that you'll open that box and ask me to marry you, and I'll...I'll just nicely say "yes," and then I'll be nice for life.

(Beat)

I'll be singing "cumbaya" for the rest of my days. I'll give back to the community, to the Salvation Army, to The MAKE A WISH FOUNDATION! And I'll do it annonymously.

(Beat)

And then one day, years from now, I'll wake up and I'll have the horrible realization that I lived a good life—that I contributed.

(Beat)

Please, for the love of God, put that box away. I mean, the planet already has millions of nice people. It doesn't need me too. I am a bitch! And I want to stay that way! Please, stop, don't—I'm asking you – No, I'm begging you – I'm getting down on my knees.

(Beat)

Will you please, please not marry me?

(Beat)

Yeah.   Well he proposed anyway.

(Beat)

And I … it felt like someone else saying it. But I heard my voice and it said …

(Beat)

Yes.

CHARLES

Cynthia wasn't really a bitch.   Those of us who knew her in the meetings, we all saw who she really was. But this man in her life – he was the first person who she loved … who got to see that side.   But as their wedding date approached, he saw it less and less ….

(Beat)

One night, after a meeting, wanting to avoid the hell that had become my home life, I asked Cynthia if I could crash on her couch and she agreed. Her fiancé had moved in with her by then and when I arrived he had this gift for her. A bottle of her favorite fragrance. Rose water perfume.

(Beat)

She freaked out.

CYNTHIA

God damn you! Stop being so thoughtful you little thoughtful fucker!

CHARLES

She hurled the perfume at him. He dodged it but it smashed against the wall and splashed all over me. I decided not to stay that night. I realized she really was the same as me ...
(Beat)
The day after she was married, she called me. She said she needed to talk. So I met her for lunch.

CYNTHIA

Oh god, Charles. I'm so, so scared. It's not too late to get it annulled I should tell him ... he and I should annul... Please ... Charles. You are like me. Maybe we ... we aren't meant to be coupled. Maybe it's not healthy for us? I don't... I really don't feel good.

CHARLES

And I – I said.
(Beat)
You can do this, Cynthia. Look, I know it can be tough, it can hurt but... But this is what we need to do to fix ourselves, right? To overcome our commitment phobias, to heal, right? We need to commit.
(Beat)
We need to really commit. Now go back to him.
(Exit Cynthia)
And had she made it back to him – he would have greeted her with open arms. Not hurt her.
(Beat)
The truth will come out, they'll let him go. He's no more guilty than I am. They're grasping at straws because they cannot fathom how a perfectly healthy young woman like Cynthia could just ... drop dead.
(Beat)
But at the end of the day, I know they're going to find that the massive coronary she suffered was caused by nothing more and nothing less than simple fright. She was literally frightened to death of committing.
(Beat)

If anyone is to blame, it's all of us who met together week after week, encouraging her and each other to heal.
>   (Beat)
I see many of you from our CPA group here today.   I won't out you, well...maybe that guy ...
>   (Points to someone in audience)
But you know who you are – oh my fellow CPAs – and if there is anything we can learn from Cynthia's death it's that maybe ... just maybe we have it all wrong.
>   (Beat)
Maybe we're not broken.   Maybe we just are this way and we should accept it, not try to change it.   Just be the emotional nomads we were born to be and be proud of it.
>   (Beat)
Because the truth is ... the truth is ... we are right to be scared, terrified, petrified of this.
>   (Holds up his hand, points to the ring on his finger....beat)
How many more Cynthia's have to die in order for us to wake-up?
>   (Beat)
Ladies and Gentleman.   My fellow CPA members.   You will not see me at our next meeting.
>   (Beat)
I quite.

                              BARB
Well, well, well.   I assume you talked to him.

                              JILL
He saw me. Came over.

                              CHARLES
Now you know the truth.

                              JILL
You let me think you were cheating with her.

                              CHARLES
I thought maybe it would make it easier for you to sign.

                              JILL

Where have you been? I was worried.

CHARLES

When I found out she died I ... I was really panicked. How much longer did – do I have? So long as we are bound in matrimony, I'm at risk.

JILL

You're not being rational.

CHARLES

Just the same. That's how I feel. I've talked to a lawyer and he's informed me I can proceed with ... or without your cooperation. It will just ... take a little longer.

JILL

You don't have to wait.

CHARLES

I don't?

JILL

I didn't actually eat the divorce papers.

CHARLES

I know. You hate ketchup.

BARB

You let him go?

JILL

I realized he was "like her." To broken to fix.
        (Beat)
I took him back to my place. I took out the papers and I signed them. You should have seen him, Barb. When I handed him the signed papers. Like a great weight had been lifted. And he said.

CHARLES

Oh Jill darling, thank you. Thank you. Thank you, darling.

JILL

And he looked at me with … love again. And he said –

CHARLES

Now we can go back to how we used to be.

BARB

He still wants to be together?
        (Jill nods)

JILL

Charles, no…

BARB

No?

JILL

No. I want – Barb you weren't wrong to push us … well to push me to marry. I wanted that. You know me. I need that and he … I guess he needs the opposite.

CHARLES

Yes.

JILL

So even though I do love him, I do love you, Charles.

CHARLES

I know.

JILL

I can't just "go back" to the way things were.
        (Beat)
As much as I hated the thought of losing him…. I need commitment.

BARB

Ok.

CHARLES

I understand.

JILL

So I promise you, darling, I won't fink out on us again.   I'll be here for you,
week in and week out for coffee, just like we used to.
        (Beat)
Because I cannot, I do not blame you for trying to give me what I wanted.
You just didn't have the power to do it.

BARB

No matter how much I nagged, huh?

JILL

And to Charles ... I'll say ...
        (Beat)
Charles.

CHARLES

Yes dear.

JILL

You know what I'm going to say.

CHARLES

I do.
        (Beat)

BARB

Go on honey.

CHARLES

Go on.

JILL

Goodbye, Charles.
        (Beat)
Goodbye.

FIN

Printed in Great Britain
by Amazon